A Laff from Lancashire

Susan Osborne
Illustrations by Sarah Bailey Cartoons

 New Generation Publishing

Introduction

I'm a Lancashire lass, musician, artist and writer, who spent many years 'on the road' entertaining in hotels, holiday camps and on cruise ships. Despite travelling to many exotic locations, I always looked forward to coming home to the red rose county where I grew up.

Eventually, I stopped travelling and settled, in Lancashire of course, with an ambition to publish some of my 'funny poems'. So, encouraged by my husband and friends, I'd like to present my first collection, which includes a cheeky diversion into the crazy world of caving and potholing.

I hope you enjoy this compilation of humorous verse and the hilarious Sarah Bailey Cartoons which bring them to life. (She's from Somerset, but we won't dwell on that!)

Turn a few pages and 'ave a laff from Lancashire.

**THE RED ROSE
COUNTY**

Contents

Northern Lass 1

He Never Asked 3

Mum, Money and Me..7

The Soapsud Saga 9

Eee I Like a Good Book 13

Where's Mi Glasses? 16

Spy in Yer Pocket 17

Bride to Be 19

April is the Cruellest Month 20

Cellulite So What 21

From Cherry Blossom 23

Diffusion 25

A Venture Underground..27

Pot'oling Panic. A Yorkshire Tale..28

Lookin' for Crackpot 31

Not Wookey Likely! 33

Nowt 36

Sunday Mornin' Show 39

Housewife's Lament 41

Bad Hair Day 44

Just What I Always Wanted. Not...45

Nation's Exclamations 47

It's Worse Than That! 49

String 51

Outdoor Pursuits 52

William Street..55

Northern Lass

I'm a Northern lass, born and bred,
Dance wi' mi feet, think wi' mi 'ead.
Dunk mi biscuits in mi tea,
And eat spud pies wi' mushy peas.

Played in back streets, on cobbles o' course!
And followed rag and bone man's cart an' 'orse.
In later years, I travelled the world,
I've seen a lot, for a Northern girl.

Caribbean islands, turquoise seas,
Ruby red sunsets, swaying palm trees,
Across the equator, through Panama Canal,
And up the mighty Amazon as well!

But pull of 'ome was strong indeed,
Cos cruisin' seven seas turned me green.
Couldn't face canapés an' caviar,
Baked Alaska or steak tartar.

I fancied black puddin' and tripe 'n' chips,
But oceans motions made me feel sick.
Longing to be somewhere else instead,
Thoughts of Lancashire filled mi 'ead.

So I set off back and was 'orrified
At mi motorway breakfast wi' black pud, FRIED!
Sliced and fried, is a downright sin.
Black puddin' should be BOILED, in its skin!

Back in Lancs, at last I'm 'ome.
I no longer feel the need to roam.
I can travel in thought, from mi chair, wi' a brew,
Smile, and dunk another biscuit…..or two….

He Never Asked

'How old? I never would have guessed!'
This genuine surprise sparks a massive cheesy grin,
Widening with flattery, threatening to reach both ears.
I try not to look too pleased, cos, this happens a lot and
Though I'm really dead chuffed, I pretend I'm not.

There was one time though, not too long ago
On day out, that left me feelin' pretty low.
Brother, girlfriend, mum and me,
Set out to put tic-tac boys through their paces,
For mum's birthday trip, to Beverley Races.

We stopped at a pub to have lunch on the way,
A cracking start to our horsey day, but
Shame about the weather, it should've been dry.
Weather forecast was wrong for a change,
We spent most of t' day under brollies in t' rain.

We had to go through turnstiles to pay.
Mum made a bee-line for t' pensioners one,
Brother and girlfriend headed for t' other.
Bringing up the rear, I stopped for a programme,
Cos no-one else 'ad bothered to buy one!

'How old should you be for t' cheaper rate?'
I heard mum ask this chap on t' gate.
'Sixty,' he said, so she grabbed mi arm,
Pulling me behind her, in t' **pensioners** queue.
I hid mi alarm in a fake smile, like you do.

Mum went through and I was next.
He never asked mi age, I presumed he would.
I could hardly speak, so I stood and looked
Into his face, but not a flicker or a trace of doubt,
'Ten pound please,' was all that came out.

I did a fish-impression, ticket in hand,
Wanting to bury mi 'ead in t' sand.
I pushed the bar, all flushed and embarrassed.
'Should've gone to Specsavers,' I mumbled as I passed.
I couldn't believe, **he never asked!**

At the show ring, Mum fancied this 'orse.
She said it winked at 'er as it passed. Yeah, course!
It started to rain and I knew it liked wet
So I thought it might make a savvy first bet,
Despite the fact, **he never asked**!

We walked to t' finishing post, stood at rails,
Feelin' all excited, I bit me nails,
Battlin' down t' straight, we cheered Dobbin on,
Jumpin' up and down like loonies when he won!
But mi smile didn't last, cos **he never asked**.

We collected our winnings, then it rained some more,
So out came brollies, still wet from before.
Coffee stand by t' Tote was our shelter till it passed.
Winnings bought hot drinks and cakes,
That tasted great, tho **he never asked**.

We backed winners and losers and had a great trip,
Drank hot chocolate in t' rain, shared a bag o' chips,
Laughed out loud when our horse came last,
But on t' way 'ome, I 'ad a painful vision
Of big knickers, bingo and a bus-pass,
Cos, **he never asked**. . . . .

. . . . **HE NEVER ASKED!**

Mum, Money and Me

'I'll get this!' 'No you won't!'
'You paid last time, it's my turn today.'
We jostle for position as we near the till,
She's a little old dear, with a stubborn strong will.
I'm trying in vain to teach her a lesson,
Paying for my time shouldn't be her obsession.
I do it for nowt and I'll gladly pay
For hot chocolate and carrot cake, any day.

We sit at a table, goodies on our tray,
And I'm thinking of ways to trick her, and pay
Our bill before she grabs her purse.
She offers some money, I try not to curse!
While I'm droolin' over lemon meringue pie,
She waves to the waitress and catches her eye,
Whips out her card with speedy stealth,
And pays up before I can empty my mouth.

I object, 'Hey! You shouldn't have done that!'
She gives me a grin like a Cheshire cat.
This time she's won, I look her in the eye.
She beat me to it, she'd old, but fly.
Next time, I tell her I need the loo.
It's a good trick. I've got one or two!
I sneak by the till and before she sees,
I pay our bill, nice as you please!

But I don't always win this battle,
She has her own sneaky ways to tackle
This familiar race to settle up,
Before t' other of us can finish up.
I reckon for her it's a bit of fun,
Squabblin' over a currant bun.
But Mum, don't bother who pays or how much,
Eat up, sup up, then GO DUTCH!

The Soapsud Saga

A massive grin, swelled with grown-upness,
At the tender age of nearly ten,
Cos I was allowed to do washing up,
Supervised by mi Gran, who lived with us then.

The other sibling couldn't be trusted
With knives, forks, glasses and hot water.
He was way too young, and besides,
I was the grown-up eldest daughter.

I took great delight in telling mi brother
He wasn't allowed, cos he was too small.
So, he wasn't impressed when I stood on t' foot stool.
Well, at nearly ten, I wasn't that tall.

But I was happy, up to mi elbows in suds,
Giving plates a good old scrub,
Then passing to Gran, who was waiting to dry
And throw back any rejects that caught her eye.

By 'eck, she was quick to spot bits I'd missed,
Tossing 'em back with a tut as she did.
I felt a bit miffed, but I scrubbed them again,
Till everything was spotless and me nearly ten.

By the time I was twelve, starry-eyed willingness
To rush to mi job at t' kitchen sink
Had somehow become a daily chore.
I wanted to play out, not be grown up any more.

But brother, nearly ten, offered some respite.
'He could do it now!' I thought, with delight.
Apparently, men and boys don't wash up in our house.
'It's women's work,' said Gran, so I shut mi mouth!

Wouldn't fancy her chances with that excuse today,
But I accepted mi lot, reluctantly,
With a scowl for mi snotty-nosed little bro,
Who smirked and went to play with his pal up the road.

Some days, depending what we had for tea,
A dreaded baked-on oven dish hid among the plates.
All I wanted was to be out with mi mates,
Off on our bikes, but I knew they wouldn't wait.

So I rubbed and scrubbed, getting worked up and mad,
Till good old Gran passed me a Brillo Pad.
Oozing suds in a pretty shade of pink,
A wire wool, shredded wheat, magic weapon at the sink.

No non-stick technology in our house then,
It was all elbow grease and gritted teeth,
Laced with a dose of soapy frustration,
Long before Teflon had gripped the nation.

At fourteen, Gran was no longer by mi side.
'She's gone to Heaven.' They meant, she'd died.
I missed her a lot and mi daily chore
Was a constant reminder she was with me no more.

Lots changed after Gran was gone.
More siblings to deal with and more dirty plates.
The Fairy Liquid was running out fast
And some of our house rules belonged in the past.

One day, mi cloud got a silver lining,
When twelve year-old bro got told to wash up!
Supervising and drying became mi new chore,
Which made him hate me even more.

'You've missed a bit!' I was just like Gran,
Tossing back the frying pan.
It made a splash that hit him in th' eye,
So he ran off to mum, pretending to cry.

Good ploy! Got him off t' hook, no messin'.
He sat by t' telly watching Batman and Robin
While I finished on mi own, but I didn't mind.
I was bossy, nearly fifteen, but not unkind.

At seventeen, washing up was a proper bind,
Shortening time in t' park with mi friends.
Eyeing up boys, reading magazines, putting make-up on,
Doing home-work and falling in love with Donny Osmond.

Mi younger sister was new recruit then,
Standing on t' foot stool, just as I'd done before.
Feeling grown up, bonding in our domestic chore.
Everything was spick and span, we even mopped t' floor.

Here I am, years later, at mi very own kitchen sink,
Remembering all those soapsuds from mi past.
I look at mi dirty dishes, then grin, cos I'm not daft,
I just chuck 'em in mi dishwasher and LAFF!

Eee I Like a Good Book

Eee I like a good book.
Books fill my shelves, covered in dust,
Stand in piles under my bed,
Invading my stairs. Every tread
Is only half the width it should be,
As I climb up to bed with my cup of tea
And my chosen tome, by title took
From a dusty shelf. Eee I like a good book!

Eee I like a good book
For holidays, exotic trips far away.
Fantasy island, palm trees, beach,
Better to relax in with good books to read.
Novels, biographies, murders, romance,
Politicians, magicians, all of them dance
In a world of words. Kings, villains, cooks,
Love 'em all. Eee I like a good book!

Eee I like a good book,
But I'm running out of space.
Millions of words, all over the place.
Even put shelves in the downstairs loo,
Cos it's good to read, or sit and do
A Sudoku or two, and finally admit
To a hard back obsession, a library look
Of paper pillars. Eee I like a good book.

Eee I like a good book,
But there's room no more,
I can hardly move when I open my door.
Piles of 'em everywhere, all must go.
I filled my car, front and back seats and boot,
Stopping at titles, with a fond lingering look.
I said goodbye, and hands I shook
With the charity shop keeper. Eee I like a good book.

Eee I like a good book,
But now they're all gone,
I have space to dance and let in the sun.
The dusty, musty smells have faded,
Sunlight gate crashes where books once shaded.
But I smile, relax and put my feet up,
Admiring my new-found de-cluttered look,
No more books! Eee I like a good E-book!

Where's Mi Glasses?

They're round 'ere somewhere, just 'ad 'em in mi 'and.
Must have put 'em down. I really don't understand
How they could 'ave disappeared right before mi eyes.
Could 'ave sworn they'd be in 'ere, I really am surprised.

Can't see 'em anywhere, thought I'd put 'em on mi desk,
But if I had, I couldn't see 'em, this is such a mess!
Feeling about makin' targets of anything that shines,
But everything's so fuzzy with eyes as bad as mine.

A stapler, a paper clip, some scissors and some keys,
Owt but mi glasses. Oh give me strength, please!
Back-track, think, 'Now where 'ave I just been?'
Garden shed, bathroom, kitchen, I could scream.

I can't keep making circles in out-of-focus space,
With a screwed up, swallowed-a-wasp, sorry, frowning face.
Pointless squinty searches fill me full o' dread.
Hands raised up, I give up, then find 'em, on mi 'ead!

Spy in Yer Pocket

Server says I've used all mi data,
I look at t' screen in disbelief.
Who's countin'? Where's calculator?
I can do wi' out this grief!
I'm supposed to 'ave five mega thingies
I can't 'ave used 'em all,
And 'ow much is this gonna cost
Every time I make a call?

I've 'ad mi fill of apps and uploads,
Downloads and messages on t' screen,
Annoying aids like predictive text
Using spellings I've never seen!
'Just sit quietly in mi pocket
And ring when mi friends want a chat.
Don't bother me wi' t' other stuff
Cos I'm proper sick o' that.'

It knows every 'igh street shop I pass,
Even tho' I never went in.
So, 'how was your coffee in Starbuck's?' It asks.
'Well, 'ow d' yer know I've bin?'
On foot, by car, or take the train
It knows mi every move.
Notifications and information,
Mi privacy's bein' abused!

And while I'm at it, tell me why
'The Cloud' isn't really in the sky,
Nor is 'Bluetooth' coloured blue,
But it can spy on me and you!
So where do all t' ones and zeros go
When flyin' through our space?
Savin' data and information
And storin' it someplace?

Who's collectin' all this data?
And wher's this mystery stash?
Will it come back to haunt me later?
Will a cyber thief nick mi cash?
If I wer you I'd be real suspicious
Switch off, use a passcode, block it,
Before yer buy summat cheap from China,
Courtesy of the SPY IN YER POCKET!

Bride to Be

Something old, something new
Something borrowed, something blue.
Got most of that, just one remains.
Think some more, oh my, the pain!

I have a ring mum gifted me,
With a sapphire as blue as blue can be.
Sherry will lend me her Montblanc pen.
I've never written with one of them!

So, I have the blue and the borrowed too,
My outfit is lovely and all brand new.
Something old I have to find
Not that easy, what a bind!

Something old, something new,
Something borrowed, something blue.
I frown, I think, Eureka! Light glitters.
I'll wear a pair of my old knickers!

April is the Cruellest Month

Wind is fierce, rain's lashin' down,
I'm inside lookin' out, wearin' a frown.
Brave young shoots battered to death,
I heave a sigh and watch mi breath
Mist over t' glass as I sip mi brew,
Peerin' at the sorry, soggy view.

So much for Spring! Can't cut mi grass,
Mi lawn's like a sponge and I'm sat on mi....OH!
Mi poor daffs! Robbed of golden splendour,
Lyin' in t 'mud like wounded soldiers.
Battle weary and bleedin' out,
Was it worth it? Did they ever doubt?

All those lives, so young, so bold,
Watchin' t' rain. Damn! Mi tea's gone cold!

Cellulite So What

I'm standing in front of a tall mirror,
Something I do quite a lot. Distracted
By my lemon shower gel aroma,
Pampered, towelled and scrubbed.

Body-brushed, glowing orange-peel skin.
Feeling fruity, with a tempting wiggle,
Reflection's no lie and it's sure not thin.
Dimply bottom wobbles, I have to giggle.

Nostrils filled with fruitiness, I see
Pale skin, squidgy and rutted,
No velvety pretty peaches for me,
But cellulite, and for a moment, I'm gutted!

Peering at the fleshy sight,
I twist and turn and crick my neck.
Holding in and squeezing tight,
I frown at the mirror. Oh what the heck!

Who's to say how I should be?
With chin up in defiance, this is me!
I hurry and dress, give my hair a rake,
Thinking, 'Sod the cellulite, I'm off to eat cake!'

From Cherry Blossom

Here 'e comes, still on a leash,
On t' dreaded morning walk.
I know he'll stop, he always does,
While 'is owner waits and talks.
Ooh! 'ang on! 'Ere's somethin' new,
Stopped at Laburnum fer a change.
But not fer long, 'e carries on
And 'eads toward me again.

Trouble is, as soon as he's done
Rest will all follow suit.
One by one they'll cock their legs,
Till I'm soaked, right down to mi roots.
I'm planted beside t' bench you see,
Where everyone stops to chat.
They don't seem to notice t' foul smell o' pee,
As they talk about this and that.

I look down t 'path at Laburnum,
Bright yellow with lovely scent,
I envy 'im that position
Away from t' dog-walkers' bench.
I pray they'll take some pity fer once,
And walk their dogs on by.
Let 'em piddle on Rhododendron,
Or give th 'Orse Chestnuts a try!

There's gateposts, lamp posts, railings an' all,
Plenty of places to pick,
But one stops 'ere and rest all come
To tiddle on mi trunk till I'm sick!
So please folks 'ave a thought fer me
When you bring yer dogs to t' park,
Guide 'em to another tree
And spare me pee-soaked bark!

Diffusion

If I were an Aboriginal Australian,
I would walk off into the desert sunset and never look back,

But I'm not.
I would blister and burn my feet on the hot dusty earth.

If I were a helicopter pilot,
I would take off into the sky and dance with migrating birds,

But I'm not.
I would crash land and break my bones on the rocks below.

If I were a warrior,
I would don my armour with sword and shield and fight off the
enemy,

But I'm not.
I'd fall at the first challenge and lie wounded on the grass.

If I were a princess,
I would wear a sparkly floaty dress and have magical powers.

I wish!
Then I would wave my wand and make it all better.

A Venture Underground

Under the protective eye of my caver husband, my first venture underground felt like playing 'Tomb Raider', or being an extra in, 'Journey to the Centre of the Earth!' It definitely had a 'wow' factor. So I joined the club!

Hopefully, I won't offend caving buddies at Red Rose Cave and Pothole Club with my cheeky beginner's look at their sport.

It is essential to wear the 'right gear' of course, which loosely consists of a woolly onesie under caving overalls, the all-important torch-bearing helmet to light the way, knee pads for crawling through narrow passages, plus various harnesses ropes and ladders to help you safely descend death-defying routes, wearing wellies for the wet, muddy terrain below.

If my flippant look at this odd activity doesn't put you off, I can recommend the organised chair winch into Gaping Gill in the Yorkshire Dales, which will safely transport you 98 metres down into the largest underground cavern in the country.

The next section has a bit of a 'laff' at cavers and their antics. 'Sunday Mornin' Show', ridiculous as it seems, is actually based on a true story. No wonder folk think cavers are a weird bunch!

Pot'oling Panic. A Yorkshire Tale

Primed and ready in all t' right gear,
Top to toe and ear to ear.
Feeling like Noddy in red and bright blue,
Wi' dazzling green wellies and an 'elmet that's new.

Oversuit's like tarp, so walkin' is tough,
Wi' harness and cow's tails, you'd think that's enough,
But noooo! There's bags of ladders and ropes.
It's a long way down, there's a lump in mi throat!

'Reet, down tha goes,' he pointed to me.
A ruddy great 'ole is all I can see.
Looking fearless, well, doin' mi best,
I 'ead fer t' 'ole, beginnin' to sweat.

Down that ladder slowly I go
One step at a time, in to t' darkness below.
Cold water's drippin' splish splash plop,
Mi breath is quickenin' I'll 'ave to stop.

I'm swingin' about, lookin' around.
It's a long way back up, and a long way down.
Inside mi gloves, mi knuckles are white,
Shakin in mi wellies, I'm 'angin' on tight.

Blimey who's that, zippin' right by?
Abseilin' in from up in t' sky.
Bloody show-off, looks easy, I'm sure.
I'm still climbin' down, but I can't see a floor.

'Keep on comin',' he shouts from below.
'Just a bit further, not far to go.'
I'm doin' mi best but I'm stuck to t' ladder,
It's worse than that, I've got a weak bladder!

I can't cross mi legs while I'm 'angin' on.
'Yer'll 'ave to move, come on, come on!'
'I'm comin' I'm comin', give us a sec.'
I finally make it and land in t'wet.

So, I'm sat in this stream bed, deep down in t' dark,
Folk do this fer fun, sod that fer a lark!
There's a light on mi 'ead and I'm soakin' wet,
I knew I shouldn't 'ave taken that bet!

I thought this water would be cold as ice,
But where I'm sat it's warm and nice.
I might 'ave guessed, good job they can't see,
It's only warm cos I've just 'ad a pee!

Lookin' for Crackpot

A couple of cavers went looking for Crackpot.
'I've been down it before, I know where it is.'
So spoke Bill who forgot to say
It was thirty-odd years ago, not yesterday!

We parked the car and started to walk.
'It's near that clump of trees over there.'
It didn't look far, so I followed along,
Though the track was narrow and muddy, and long!

Some trail bike rider had carved up the path,
It made me feel angry as I hugged the wall,
Trying to manoeuvre a slippery slope,
Wondering how the Hell that biker had coped!

He must have been close to Olympic standard
And even though I admired his skill
At riding this narrow, slippery path,
His reckless behaviour filled me with wrath!

Muddy tyre marks took our attention,
So we didn't notice the angle iron posts
That marked a steep route down to the cave.
Later, we counted the miles we'd have saved!

Onwards and downwards and into the valley,
Slipping on the muddy route.
Grabbing rocks, getting spiked by thorns,
Trying not to fall, or get trousers torn!

'Oh look! The entrance is up there,' said Bill.
And sure enough I could see it well,
High above a pile of moss covered boulders.
We had to climb, I shrugged mi shoulders!

We scrambled up toward the entrance,
Only to find it collapsed, and blocked
By fallen rocks and a resting owl, who took flight
Close to Bill's head and gave him a fright!

A few yards to the left was a smaller entrance,
Still accessible, though you'd have to crawl.
Bill said, 'This is one we could do.
A nice easy cave for a shorthouse like you!'

So it's on the list for another visit,
To brave the steep path marked by iron posts,
In our wellies, and jump suits, helmets and all
And kneepads of course, for the knee-wrecker crawl!

Not Wookey Likely!

Booked a couple of nights at Wessex C.C.
Plenty in the area to do and see,
A friendly welcome, a cup of tea,
Ready for some site seeing Bill and me.
Up at crack 'o dawn to check our maps,
(Ok, mid-morning) Glastonbury Tor up for grabs.
So, up we went and up some more
Till we reached the top, great views galore!

Business took us near Shaftesbury.
Well, it's Hovis land, so it 'ad to be
Gold Hill, as steep as the telly ad said,
Plus a giant Hovis statue, we could fair smell 'ot bread.
We walked t' steep cobbles, in bare feet o' course,
No 'and cart for us, no bicycles, no 'orse,
And no fresh baked 'ovis and no cup o' tea,
But a beautiful vista for Bill and me.

Not far from Cheddar, great Gorge an' all,
We opted for a trip down Wookey Hole.
Of course the place was a doddle to find
But it weren't the cavin' we 'ad in mind.
For a start it were twenty quid a-piece.
'Flippin' Eck! 'Ow much?' We couldn't believe
What a rip off! A tourist price, all in
With Dinosaur Park, Pirates and paper makin'!

Paper Making? Yep! That's what's on offer,
Not an attraction for a caver proper.
Needless to say, second thoughts caught us,
Didn't fancy hot dogs with Brontosaurus.
The place was more like a Holiday Camp,
We were hoping for something cold and damp,
Not Gladys from Heidi Hi, oh crikey!
Did we go in then? Not Wookey likely!

This next verse is dedicated to Jim Newton, one of the oldest members of Red Rose Cave and Pothole Club and respected long time caver and digger, famous for his part in the 1970 British Speleological Expedition to the Himalayas, in a double decker bus! His tales and slide shows have entertained members on many a social gathering at Red Rose HQ, Bull Pot Farm.

Nowt

Nowt's new fer Newton
'E's done it all before.
So, you're camping at the farm now?
Well, 'e was there in '64.

'Which cave was that?' I heard him say,
'I remember when I had a look,'
And he'll wind back the years with 'is gripping yarns
And 'is mem'ries, 'is jokes and 'is book.

And as for that big adventure
In a handsome red double-decked bus,
Made 'Summer Holiday' look like a toddler's trip,
No offence Cliff, don't make a fuss.

Through Iran, Afghanistan, Pakistan,
And the infamous Khyber pass,
More than five thousand miles, Jim n 'is pals
Bussed it to the Himalayas!

From desert heat to snow-capped peaks,
Jim was young and in 'is prime,
Daring and brave, exploring new caves,
Makin' mem'ries to last a lifetime.

Now, he's a sweet old Granddad,
With a constant cheery grin,
But 'e's bin a lion of a lad underground
Finding new 'oles and diggin'.

I've said it before and I'll say it again,
Ole Jim's got tales a-plenty
Just start 'im up and let 'im go
The banter's never empty.

Long before your LED's
With 'is stinky 'e went below.
Carbide back then, not batteries,
Would light the way to go.

You might 'ave been a nipper
Sat on yer mammy's knee,
But 'e was already down the 'ole
Wi' a couple o' cavers or three.

Has 'e bin here? Has 'e bin there?
Well, I daresay 'e's bin in 'em all.
'E remembers 'em well and will tell you the way
Wi' great detail and a few jokes an' all.

Over Yorkshire Dales and far beyond
Old Jim's bin down 'oles galore,
And if you think you've found a new un,
I'll bet Jim was there before!

Sunday Mornin' Show

It was a crisp spring day and two old dears
Sat cosily in their car.
Tea cups in hand and newspapers too,
They hadn't travelled far,

A regular jolly on a Sunday morn,
They enjoyed the peace and quiet.
They sat and read, looking o're them hills
That view! You couldn't buy it.

Cavers pulled up, paying little heed,
And parked their van as planned.
They all made haste, done this before,
Rope bags and helmets in hand.

Woolly bears, oversuits, wellies and all,
The banter was lively as can be.
They took off their trousers and started to change,
Didn't notice th' old dears could see!

Oh my, all that flesh, what a sight for sore eyes!
Jockies off and flung into t' van.
Before donning gear to take them below,
They were naked, every last man.

Well, Ethel and Alice (whatever their names)
Had dropped their newspapers fast,
Took off reading glasses and peered outside
With grins like Cheshire cats.

'Thanks fer t' full Monty,' they shouted out.
The lads turned and gave them a wave.
'Hope you're coming back next week,
You've really made our day!'

Housewife's Lament

I've hardly slept these past few nights.
Mi back aches, and mi bra's too tight.
If I had the strength I'd be flamin' mad,
But I'm just too tired....it's very sad!
Why am I at the end of mi tether?
I'll tell you, seeing as we're all together.

Five days ago today, arrived the cause of mi dismay.
With his black box of tricks and some wires as well,
This bloke marched up mi path, and rang mi bell!
'Where d' ya want it luv?' he said with a grin.
I said, 'Don't you be so cheeky young man!'
Then, I let him in.

My Joe was there, fat lazy slob!
Sprawled on the couch, playing with his Xbox
He was that excited he jumped to his feet.
That's novel for him, he's usually glued to that seat.
He greeted this chap, he was so pleased to see,
And packed me off, to make us some tea.

In no time at all, the job was done,
And we all had a brew, and a buttered currant bun.
Then I saw it! This thing I've grown to hate,
Lurking among the crumbs on Joe's empty plate.
Not much to look at, in fact quite small.
That bloody TV REMOTE CONTROL!

Well! I can't watch telly no more.
Coronation Street, East Enders, Emmerdale Farm,
All disappear in a 'click',
From this new extension to Joe's arm.
Up at all hours, flick flick flick,
Forever changing channel, I'm sick sick sick!

Last night, I thought 'Enough! Time for action.'
I flew upstairs, splashed on mi Fatal Attraction.
Under mi dressing gown, corset, stockings, the lot,
I slunk into the lounge, and picked me spot.
Joe held the remote but he soon turned round
When I slipped off the fluffy towelling gown.

I have to admit, God I was hot!
As it fell to the floor, his jaw fair dropped.
His eyes were all over me, he licked his lips,
Thank you Red Tube for the sexy hot tips!

I shimmied toward the couch with me proposition……
'Tonight Joe …. How d'ya fancy a new position?'
'Coooorrrrrr! I'm game luv, you know me!'
I took the remote, smiling sweet as can be,
Then yelled, 'GET BEHIND THAT IRONING BOARD
WHILE I WATCH TV!'

Bad Hair Day

I pick up my hairbrush and brush my hair,
It's the first thing I do when I get out of bed.

Throughout the day, if I see a stray hair,
I pick up my hairbrush and brush my hair.

Not short of obsessive, in mirrors I stare,
If I think it's untidy I'm filled with dread,

I pick up my hairbrush and brush my hair,
It's the last thing I do before going to bed.

Just What I Always Wanted. Not

Sparkly paper rustles and tears.
Eager eyes watch my face.
Something soft and pink revealed,
But on my face not a trace
Of the 'Oh no! Yuk! I hate it!'
Hide that thought, smile, look elated.

He didn't notice the split-second blip
That would have told him, I'm about to lie
Through my teeth as I give him a hug.
Over his shoulder my eyes reach the sky,
And I wonder why he still doesn't know
That I hate bloody pink and I'm never gonna wear it, so....

What do I say? 'It's lovely, fab colour!'
No, that's too much, he might twig.
I'll have to think of something else,
I shouldn't tell a lie that big!
Don't mention colour, that's a better idea,
And whisper sweet nothings in his ear.

He probably tried his best, I'm sure,
Torturing himself, choosing from the shelf.
A neutral colour would have been nice,
Or a pair of socks, or a Santa Elf!
At least he didn't throw me some money
And send me off with a 'Treat yourself honey!'

No, give him his due, he made an effort,
Worth far more than a girlie pink sweater.
If I drop enough hints, in a future endeavour
He might actually choose something better
Suited to my tastes, but what the Hell,
He probably hates his Christmas jumper as well!

Nation's Exclamations

Sat in the caf' with a brew an' cake,
Surrounded by folk from all over t' place.
East, west, north and south,
Local riddles from every mouth.

Corr blimey! Wotcha cock,
Slippery eel, set the clock.
Keep tha shirt on, get ready to rock.
Now it's time to tie the knot.

Shiver me timbers, brass monkeys an' all
Me throat's parched, he's not playing ball.
A bird in the hand, strike up the band
Walking on air, aint life grand.

Boilin' mad, it aint that bad,
Put wood in th' hole, it could've bin worse,
Whistle and flute, apples and pears,
Well I'll go to t' foot of our stairs.

Whose coat is that jacket?
Designer label Boyo, cost a packet.
Top o' the mornin' and how d'ya do?
Stick it in reverse, the same to you,

Guts for garters I'm in a spin,
Why aye man, when the boat comes in,
Tak a wee dram, hock aye the noo.
Feelin' grand and dinky doo.

I supped me tea and do declare,
I've never heard such blummin twoddle,
Shut tha' cakehole, it's rude to stare,
So I left the caf' with mi 'ead in a muddle!

It's Worse Than That!

I ambled along the path
Through the park on a wintry day,
It was crisp and fresh and filled with joy,
I sang along the way.
'Mornin,' said I,
To dog walkers passing by.
'Good morning,' smiles and wagging tails
Came back to me, as I followed the trail.

Through frosted branches
Peered wintry sun,
Pale yellow blur in a grey, grey sky,
Enough to cast a sparkle on the brook nearby,
Enough to make me smile
As I listened to its tune,
Tumbling over rocks and roots
Down a gully full of young green shoots.

Through the woods the track went on,
Following the stream's trickling song.
A chill in the air, I had not one care,
Then it happened ... 'Oh No!
Don't let this be!'
I bet you're thinking I needed a pee.
With no place to hide in this popular spot,
I'd be in a right pickle ... except I'm not.

In the great outdoors there's always a risk
That Nature will teach you a lesson,
And today was my turn, it had to come,
It will leave a lasting impression.
Tho' it's been the ill fate of many,
The thought always filled me with dread,
And on this glorious day, no hat, no hood,
A bird went and pooped on mi 'ead!

String

String, string, strrrrrring!
    It has quite a ring
        To it.
            You can do so many things
        With it.
      Fantastic to see
    How manipulated string
  Can be.
Discover the art of
      Macramé.
            Possibilities are lots,
                Japanese art of tying
                    Knots
           To make pretty hangers
        For pots,
      Planted with trailing ivy
        And pretty forget me nots,
              Blue,
          In various terracotta pots,
        Not new.
To make headbands and belts
      Decorated with beads,
           To sell
           To long-haired hippies. Ting!
        Finger bell.
     Knotted with sea shells,
   Lots of beaded tassels
      That Swish.
           Songs of 'peace and love man.'
              Wish!

Outdoor Pursuits

Being an outdoorsy type
Of a certain age, (hush hush),
Means yer can't last an entire hike
Bowt needin' an 'andy bush.
But when dancin' o'er cobbled paths,
Cos t' beck's makin' tinklin' sounds,
Ther's rocks and bracken, nettles and grass,
But not a single bush t' be found.

Climbin' o're a dry stone wall,
To 'opefully get out o' sight,
Being extra careful not to fall,
When t' farmer's bull gives me a fright.

Bad idea. Can't tinkle 'ere
That bull is lookin' my way,
And a quick exit wi' mi pants 'alf mast?
No chance! Not 'appenin' t'day!

Soldierin' on, ther's woods up yon,
And chance for relief in th' air.
So, t' search is on fer a big fat trunk
To 'ide mi exposed derrière.
This one might do, t' other side o' t' path,
Don't think I'll be seen from 'ere.
Am just gettin' down when I 'ears this sound
And a raggy old sheep appears.

I know it shouldn't matter, but I just can't go
Wi' t' sheep lookin' at me, nowt will flow.
So, feelin' watched, I pull up mi keks
And hunt for another place, crossin' mi legs.

Ther's sheep all o're t' shop now
And more folk on t' path, I'm upset.
I'll 'ave t' find a hiding place soon,
Or I'll get mi knickers wet.

A fallen tree is spied ahead
Just up an embankment, short climb.
I won't be seen from t' other side
I should make it just in time!
So I scrambles up that steep incline
Toward th' uprooted trunk,
Hoppin' over and crouchin' down,
Then checkin' no-one can look.

At long last after much ado,
I can finally release.
Despite the cold and tell-tale steam,
Oh boy! What a sense of relief!

And ther's mi pals waitin' patiently,
Crackin' jokes on t' path below,
I smile at them ladies of a certain age,
Won't be long till they need t' go!

Crossin' bridges and climbin' stiles
Wi' us walkin' poles we clock up miles,
Banter's lively, ther's mud on our boots,
Dartin' behind bushes along our routes.
Finally, we reach our village
And 'ead to t' caf' fer a brew,
Where one bi one we spend a penny
On a more civilized 'ow d'ya do!

William Street

Siren sounds the call to work,
Labourers in red brick dust clad.
Clogs sparking on old worn cobbles,
Harmless banter 'twixt dads and lads.

Peering through my Jack Frost hole,
William Street's all quiet now,
Till our rag and bone man rattles by
With horse and cart and rags piled high.

Coal man's next with 'is flatbed truck,
Deliverin' sacks all covered in muck.
Chimney pots smokin' o'er fire's lit below,
Fetch another bucket and SHUT THAT DOOR!.

Socks and shoes and off to school,
Down back streets with a sixpence for treats,
Stopping at sweet shop for liquorish sticks,
With my pal Lynn and her brother, Mick.

Back same route by coits and coal 'oles,
Washin' pegged on lines at our back gate.
Socks at half-mast, satchel bursting,
Hot buttered crumpet on my plate.

William Street, my Lowry land,
Two streets from t' brick yard's gate,
Where men and boys worked long and hard,
And kids like me played in the dirt.

Thank You

To my wonderful husband, who was my captive audience as I read and performed my poems out loud, edited them and then suffered him to listen all over again... and again... and again...

To all my friends at Write Lines who gave me lots of support and encouragement, and most importantly, the courage to put this first collection together,

To Sarah, of Sarah Bailey Cartoons, whose fantastic talent has enriched the comedy of my poems page after page,

To all at New Generation Publishing, who turned my scribbles into a REAL book and helped me fulfil a long held ambition,

To you, the reader, I hope you enjoyed my northern humour and hope you will come back for 'Another Laff from Lancashire.'

Susan Osborne.

THE RED ROSE COUNTY

Lightning Source UK Ltd.
Milton Keynes UK
UKHW020450250621
386095UK00007B/68